Preface

Our heavenly Father longs to have us respond to His love through the birds and animals He has given us. When Robby became a part of our life, we felt it was a gift from above. It took time and patience to gain his love and trust, but it was worth it!

The joy he gave to us with his beautiful songs and delightful "communications" must be the same joy that God must feel when we offer Him our songs, prayers, and praises of thanksgiving.

Chapter One

I stood by the window in the early morning, enjoying the fresh air and wondering what the day would bring. Little did I know that I'd remember this day, July 13, 1969, for a long, long time.

Our days were always packed with activity, as gardening and farming more than filled every hour. We had two greenhouses where we grew vegetable and flower plants. At the right time, we planted for our own use and sold the others. Our 160 acres, which we irrigated according to our needs, kept us hopping.

On this special morning we had to get an early start as we needed to hoe out the yellow mustard plants growing in our sweet-corn field. It was best to clear out the mustard while they were young and tender, before they grew a strong root system.

Looking out the window, I could see the sun just peeking over the horizon. What a beautiful sight! As it rose higher and higher, it looked like a golden ball of fire, lighting up the whole world with it's celestial glory.

I turned to awaken my sleeping husband, Tom. "Wake up," I said. "You must see this beautiful sunrise. It is too spectacular to miss." Still half-asleep, he came to the window to share in the beauty of the morning.

"We must hurry to get our day started," he told me a moment later. "Maybe we can get the mustard cleaned out of the cornfield in the cool of the day. We don't know what the afternoon will bring. It could rain before the day is over, and it would be good to have that job finished."

I never questioned Tom when he predicted the weather. I often saw him watching the clouds, and he always seemed to know what kind of weather to expect. As a young man he'd learned many things from his father. Both his father and grandfather had been commercial gardeners.

By 6:00 a.m. we were ready to begin the outside work. It took just a few minutes to sharpen the hoes, and soon we were busy cutting out the wild, yellow blossoms that had volunteered all over the cornfield.

I wasn't aware of it, but Tom was watching the sky. Suddenly he turned to me and exclaimed, "Let's get to the house right now! See that bank of clouds coming our way?"

I looked where he pointed and sure enough I saw a cloud, like a large, black blanket, rolling in our direction. It was coming fast. I didn't see a funnel, but possibly the trees hid a funnel from view.

Tom, already hurrying toward the house, turned and called back to me. "Hurry! Don't hoe any more. We don't have that much time. It's coming very fast, and I think it's a tornado."

I dropped my hoe and began to run. "I'll take care of the outside," he called, "and you take care of the house. Shut all the windows to the west and the north and leave some open on the other side so it will equalize the air pressure inside and outside. I'll take care of the other buildings and the grandchildren's billy goat staked out in the apple orchard. Hurry as fast as you can. Then go to the basement to wait until the storm is over. I'll be there as soon as possible!"

We each went our different ways to do the work that had to be done. As soon as I finished, I took the flashlight and the transistor radio and started for the basement door.

Just then the kitchen door opened and Tom dashed in. He was already soaked from the heavy, blowing rain. As he closed the door, I could see the trees bending low from the heavy wind. I'd known it was a very bad storm, but I'd had little time to watch it develop in my rush to get my work finished.

We hurried to the basement to wait for the storm to pass. We were thankful for our well-constructed farmhouse. More than 100 years old, it was built of native, unplaned oak timbers which were expected to withstand the storms of time.

We stopped to thank God for providing us with a safe place to sit out the storm, then turned on the radio to see if we could get some news regarding the weather. But all we could hear was loud cracking and snapping, so we turned it off and waited.

Our home was surrounded by large, spreading elm trees which shaded our home from the hot summer sun. From one tree a large branch stretched over the kitchen porch. On this thick branch was a small hollow where a mother robin had built her nest for several years. She'd raised several broods in the tree without any problem.

We were anxious for the storm to pass so we could see what damage it had done.

After waiting a while longer, we slipped cautiously up the stairs and listened as we cracked open the basement door. Hearing nothing, we went to the kitchen door, opened it, and looked outside.

The storm had passed, and the rain had stopped, leaving a wet, soggy mass of destruction all around the yard. So we put on our rubber boots and jackets and went out to see what we should do first.

We found the yard—neatly trimmed and green an hour before—strewn with broken branches and other debris blown in by the strong winds. As we listened we heard the sobs of nature all around us. Instead of the usual early-morning bird songs, we heard the shrill distress calls of frightened young birds. They could not understand what had happened to their mothers, who had given them so much loving care.

The tornado had come up through the pasture from the north and ripped its way through the heavily wooded section. It twisted and uprooted huge trees, making a shambles of our beautiful woods. Then it headed straight toward our home. But by the providence of God, it had lifted and cleared the two-story house, clipping off the tops of the tall, spreading elms that surrounded it. Then it roared on to level many barns along its terrible path, killing the animals housed within them.

The majestic trees, where many birds had made their nests, were now a mixed-up mess of broken wood. Twisted limbs were scattered all over the ground, and the pasture fences were broken by the weight of the branches. Our garden was covered with crushed plants and debris, and our once beautiful cornfield lay in the mud, flattened by the wind.

Tom and I looked at the elm branch above our kitchen porch. The robin's nest was gone. It lay on the ground, a little pile of mud and straw. The bodies of two baby birds lay among the mess, and the mother bird was nowhere to be found. As we stood there looking it over, feeling sad for the mother who had lost her brood, we heard a loud, frightened chirp from the deep, wet grass about 50 feet away.

We followed the cry for help. To our amazement, there in the wet, twisted grass lay one of the baby robins. Its body was covered with light fuzz. It had no feathers. Though its eyes had already opened, I knew it was only a few days old. I carefully picked it up and cupped it in my hands. Its chirping changed to a contented, grateful sound. I thought that my warm hands must have felt good to its cold body.

Now, what was I to do with this tiny, naked baby bird? First, it would have to be warmed thoroughly. We hoped it had not been chilled so badly that it would die. I thought of my gas oven. It had a pilot light and would be just warm enough to help it, but not too warm to hurt it. I went inside and I wrapped the baby in a nice, soft cloth, put it in a shoebox, and placed the shoebox in the oven. I left the door open and pondered what baby robins needed to be fed.

We searched all around the yard and beyond it for the mother robin, but couldn't find her at all. We knew that without a nest, she couldn't care for her baby anyway. The wind had blown her so far away that it was three days before she returned. We saw her come back, but she didn't rebuild her nest in the elm tree. She left, and we never saw her again.

But on that first day Tom and I looked around to determine the damage and decide what had to be done first. Our sturdy barn still stood. We were grateful we'd returned all farm machinery to the barn after using it, so it was safe.

We went out to check on the horses.

They'd been in the farthest part of the pasture, away from the storm's path, and had not even noticed the broken fences. What a blessing! We removed the broken trees lying across the fences, and repaired them as quickly as possible.

As I walked toward the house, I noticed worms lying on top of the ground. I knew it would be a good time to collect them for the baby bird that was probably very hungry by now. I gathered quite a few, but they were just a beginning. I soon discovered it had an appetite that was seldom satisfied. As the days passed, we began to call our little birdie Robby, as we did not know whether it was male or female.

He was still in the shoebox, but had worked his way out of the cloth I'd first wrapped around him. He was content when I held him in my hands and soon accepted me as the provider of his every need. A large canary cage became his "home" when he was not allowed his freedom in the kitchen. When the kitchen table was not in use, I spread newspapers on it and let him go free there. Robby soon discovered that the tabletop was his own special place and was satisfied to stay there most of the time.

Chapter Two

For the first few days Robby stayed quietly on the table without moving around too much. But soon he was most content when he was near me. I cooked our meals on a gas range so I had to be very careful that he did not flutter into the flame. His feathers were coming in nicely. It bothered him to have anyone touch his back, but he didn't mind our smoothing the feathers under his neck or on the very top of his head. It was interesting to see him develop in other ways, too. Soon the baby feather down disappeared and one by one gaily colored feathers adorned his breast. Each seemed to me as a miracle of God's love in action.

Before long Robby could fly around the kitchen. He'd fly to my shoulder, perch close to my head, and whisper right into my ear. When he stayed on the table, his large eyes focused on me, watching my every move. When he was hungry he'd let out a loud chirp, knowing I'd be there in an instant to feed him.

After his first few days with us, I had no problem getting him to open his mouth to eat. He would squat, flutter his wings, and flip his tail. This habit stayed with him the rest of his days, and we could always pick him out in a group of robins. As he opened his large yellow-lined mouth for the worms he made sounds of sheer happiness. When his tummy was filled, he closed his mouth and I knew he'd had enough. He liked whole wheat bread and milk, but otherwise the only thing we fed him was earthworms. I tried to feed him strawberries or raspberries, but he'd spit them out. I was glad that I wasn't bothered by handling worms!

Sometimes I'd inadverently move when Robby flew toward my shoulder. He'd miss his aim and land on the polished kitchen floor, sliding on the slick surface until he stopped. It never seemed to bother him. He'd just try again. He was simply a delight to me.

We always put him in the birdcage at night, and I discovered that his hearing was very good—a lot better than mine. Our bedroom was upstairs, and the moment I put my feet on the floor in the morning, he let out a loud chirp, letting me know he had heard me. He strongly insisted I come down immediately and "serve" breakfast. After that I was free to go about my morning routine.

Baby birds usually leave their nest after two weeks, so I soon realized it was time for him to be enjoying the fresh air of the outdoors. If I held my hand out to him, he'd fly to my finger, so I carried him on my finger as we went outside.

At first being outside was new to Robby and he was a bit afraid. So I took him to the backyard where we had a row of French lilacs and placed him on a small branch. He had a difficult time balancing himself on the swaying branch, but I stayed near to help if he needed me. When I started to move away, he called to me, wanting me to come back. But after a few minutes he grew brave enough to try and jump from one branch to another. Before long, he was managing very nicely alone. This was the beginning of his new freedom.

When Robby learned to fly up to the

horizontal branch above the kitchen porch, he was so excited that it was wonderful to watch. He was like a child, racing back and forth between the branches, calling to me so I would notice his accomplishment. Each day brought him new interests.

He came along with me when I went to the kitchen garden. While I worked, he'd walk up and down the rows, often darting out of sight among the plants. I kept close watch on him and if he got out of my sight I'd call his name. He always answered in a moment and came running back. But soon he'd be out hunting bugs again.

My cocker spaniel dog stayed by my side too, but she had been trained to leave Robby alone. I could see by her wagging tail that she would have enjoyed getting in-volved with his search for insects.

It wasn't long before Robby's daily trips took him farther away from the house. If he didn't return for a while, I'd go out and call him. I'd hear his answering call from far away. I'd call him again; his answer would be closer. Soon he would fly up, landing on my shoulder or on my head. He found my hair was a soft landing place.

Robby grew to like high places. He liked to perch on the peaks of the buildings or the tops of the trees. I knew he was enjoying his freedom.

About this time our three grandsons, Scott, Steve, and Brad, came to spend some time on the farm. They had a great time with Robby. They each wanted to be the one to take him outdoors in the morning, so they took turns doing it. They often played with their cars in a sandy area, and Robby thought he was a little boy too. I'd see him on their shoulders, walking in their little roads, or riding on their toy cars. He wanted to be a part of everything they did, and they were eager to include him. He was such a pleasant companion and the highlight of their summer.

Robby was still regularly coming into the house for his feedings, so I had to keep a good supply of worms on hand. When he'd see me get the spade and the pail from the pump house, he knew what I was going to do. He would go with me, either riding on my shoulder or flying a few feet ahead of me. He knew just where we were going. I'd get busy digging up worms and putting them in the pail. Sometimes I'd put one down in front of Robby, hoping he would eat it without my help. He'd push it around with his beak, but he always waited for me to hand-feed him.

Hunting worms with me seemed to be special for him, as he ate by himself when he was out in the cornfield.

One day I was so busy with farm duties that I didn't have time to dig worms. I wondered what I would do since we'd be going to church the next day and I wouldn't be able to dig any then. When Tom came home from work he told me that a boy had stopped him and wanted to sell him a large can of worms for 15 cents. That was just what we needed to last Robby over the weekend.

When Tom and I went away from the house together, we left Robby outside. It didn't take too long before he'd miss us. He was usually waiting for us in the pasture along the road and would fly close by the car as we returned. Sometimes he'd be waiting for us perched on the top of the pump house. When I got out of the car he would fly over and land on my shoulder or in my hair.

Each evening before dark, Robby flew back from his busy day to be let in the house. He felt that was his home too. He'd come inside riding on one of our shoulders or he'd walk in around our feet. We had to watch so that we wouldn't step on him. Somehow he was always confident we'd never hurt him. And, of course, we didn't.

Indoors, sometimes Robby flew into the living room and zoomed from the top of one window to another. He knew it was time for him to be fed and put to bed, and this was his way of trying to prolong his day with us. But when I held up my hand, he would fly down and let me put him in his cage.

Chapter Three

As autumn began we knew other birds were getting ready for the long migration trip south for the winter, and we wondered how we would convince Robby that he must join them. To begin, we'd have to get him to stay outside for the night—the first step toward learning to live without us. It would not be easy.

I had mixed feelings about it at that particular time as I felt it was rushing him too much. I felt Robby was not ready to be separated from us, but my husband insisted. He could not see taking the risk of having him there with us during the long Minnesota winter.

One evening, instead of letting him come inside for the night, Tom carried him out to the pine grove and placed him on a branch of a tree. It was not long before Robby was trying to come in through the closed window. We were afraid he would fly into the window and get killed so we weakened and let him in. After this happened for several nights Tom took him down into the blue spruce grove where other robins roosted and put him safely into the thick branches and left him there. It was too dark for him to see his way back to the house.

The next day we didn't see him in the tree or anyplace else, and he didn't come to the house to be fed or anything else. We felt sure an owl had gotten him and that we'd never see him again. It was three days before he returned. Then he flew to me, came into the house, and wanted me to feed him again. After his little crop was well filled, I took him back outside. He had received his share of attention and was assured of our continued love and affection. Was that what he had returned for?

We saw him a few times after that, recognizing him in a flock of robins. One day he separated himself from the flock and came close for a long conversation. It seemed he was trying to tell us of his plans to go south, but he didn't get near enough for us to touch him. This is what we wanted to happen, but it was hard to have our little friend so independent. It was October 12, 1969.

Our weather was uncertain this time of year. The temperature was falling and snow could come at any time. The birds knew when it was time to leave Minnesota for their winter home where food was available and they could stay strong and healthy, ready to return in the spring.

With the birds gone, we knew winter was on the way. Our large barn, built many years ago, did not include stanchions for cattle so we had a nice open space. We partitioned off a large area for a chicken coop, made it animal-proof, then placed bales of hay against the barn's inside walls to make it warmer in the winter. We also had a brooder house where we raised our chicks before moving them to the chicken coop. For health reasons, we fed them only vegetarian food.

We kept bales of straw stacked in the area of the barn that wasn't needed for storage and used a lot of it to cover our acres of strawberries. The straw protected them from the harsh winter. We always had a number of bales left over.

A flock of bantam chickens stayed in the barn all year—winter and summer—and we took feed and water to them every day. In the fall we built a straw-bale house inside the barn so the dogs and barn cats could have a warm place to sleep. Our dogs didn't know they were "supposed" to chase our cats, so both slept together, keeping each other warm. The bantics roosted in the higher places on rafters above the warm bales.

Our winters could be quite severe—at times temperatures falling as low as minus 35 degrees, with heavy snow. The snow-drifts were very deep, so we had to keep the ground plowed to the out-buildings. But Tom and I were used to dealing with harsh winters, for we'd always lived in Minnesota. With the arrival of springtime we knew the birds would be coming back soon. We always watched when a good south wind began to blow, knowing the birds might come in with it.

My sewing room was on the second floor above the kitchen porch with my machine by the window where I had the best light for sewing. From there I could see everything that went on in the back of the farmyard. It was near the end of March 1970, as I sat upstairs sewing, that I saw a flock of robins fly in and land in the tall elm just beyond the back of the house. As I watched to see if Robby was among them I saw all but one fly away. Then I heard Robby chirping and saw him flipping his tail in his characteristic way. I called to him from the window and hurried down to greet him. He was excited to be back and started to chatter loudly. It seemed that he always felt I could understand him so I pretended that I could, answering him in return. He stayed about five minutes and then flew away in the direction the other birds had taken.

The first few days he stayed with the flock most of the time, returning to visit me for a few minutes each day. He expected me to come and listen to him tell me what he planned to do that day and what he had done during his absence.

Chapter Four

The flock of females arrived two weeks later. Apparently Robby had already selected his mate as they spent no time in letting me know they were paired for the season. They spent most of their time together, and Robby let her know we were friends. She accepted Tom and me with some reservation.

Several old lilac bushes grew in the yard by the south side of the house. We kept the grass mowed and it looked like a park. They decided this was their special place. It was private to them, but I could see them from my living room window and could watch their courting and mating process. Robby knew we were able to watch since he had once lived inside with us. He'd sat on the window sill many times, watching the same area himself, and was not afraid to have us watch them. Soon they'd be building their first nest, but we did not know where they would put it.

One morning Robby was waiting for me as I went out the kitchen door. He flew around the south side of the house calling to me. I wondered what it was he was so interested in but did not follow. He immediately returned, called, and flew around the side of the house again. I realized then that he wanted me to follow him, and he led me to the front of the house right by the front door.

Our front porch was sheltered by many ivy vines, and he led me to them. Then he flew into the ivy vines. When I came close and carefully looked among the vines, I saw their new nest. It was about three feet from the front door, just about two feet higher than the door knob. Robby was so proud of his nest and wanted my approval. I told him what a good nest it was, and then he was satisfied. I didn't touch it; I just looked and complimented him. He wanted to share his joy with me. I wondered what they would do when the eggs were laid. I would have to wait and see.

A few days later he waited near the kitchen door, again calling for me to follow him. He showed me that they had an egg in the nest. This continued until the whole clutch was laid. After the mama bird began to set, I didn't disturb her at all. However, Robby came to find me and chat every day.

When the eggs hatched, he again met me at the kitchen door to tell me something wonderful had happened. I went out to see, and they had four little nestlings. His mate was on the telephone wire watching her brood when I came there. As I moved close to look, she grew very disturbed. She did not want me to go near her family and did not hesitate to let me know. Robby flew up on the wire next to her. I don't know what he told her, but she calmed down and from that time on she let me look at—but not touch—her little family. Each day when I went to see that nothing had been disturbed, she would watch without making any noise. Both parents kept very busy taking food to their hungry babies. They grew fast with the large number of worms being served to them.

The babies left the nest in only two weeks, as robin babies do. Then it was Robby's job to do most of the baby-sitting.

He was a watchful and demanding father. He had a big job making sure his family was kept fed and nothing happened to them.

He continued to come by for our daily conversations and soon his mate became a part of it. Later I noticed that when they were together he let her do most of the talking! He had observed me with the shotgun when I went down to the wooded area on the back 40 and realized it was something we used for safety. So when he and his mate had problems with the starlings he'd call to me. He figured I would solve the problem for him. I'd take the small 22 and shoot into the air to scare them away. That satisfied him.

When our grandchildren came to visit they were disappointed that Robby would not come down and play with them as he'd done the year before. They pleaded with me to tell him they would not hurt him. I had to explain that Robby and his mate did not understand human language, and Robby was older now with different habits.

Robby was a happy bird who sang often. He'd fly up to his favorite branch—usually a branch without leaves where he could be easily seen—and sing for about five minutes. He had begun this habit at a young age. He expressed his happiness by singing to us.

It's interesting that I could tell by his voice when it was going to rain. His song had a special ring to it then. I could hear it, although Tom could not. It always rained within 24 hours after that special song. When he sang we knew his mate was nearby, for they were always near each other.

For several years we noticed a skunk around the place, usually after dark. I knew she was around the barn sometimes, but gave her no thought as long as she did no harm. Sometimes I'd go out to the chicken coop after dark to check on things and on the way would stop at the barn to look in on the bantams. Several times as I entered the large doorway I'd see the skunk just inside the door. She apparently felt I was not going to do her harm so she would turn and walk away—and I would do the same!

We had planted an acre or more of asparagus in the main garden, but we also had a smaller patch near our larger greenhouse. This patch was approximately 30 feet by 50 feet and was convenient for us to get asparagus without going out into the larger field. It all had to be harvested each day from early spring until the middle of June.

Late one evening I needed a small cutting of asparagus, so I decided to go to the small patch. As I was working, I heard what sounded to me like a number of mice. I was puzzled, and I turned to see what it was. I saw the mother skunk about 25 feet from me. My first thought was to creep away, but on second thought I stood and watched. The sound I'd heard was the mother skunk talking to her kits who followed her in single file like a train. What a beautiful sight. I just stood there and watched her. She was showing them how to hunt for grubs as she led them out into the large field. She had delivered her babies in the barn among the straw bales and was taking them from her nest, teaching them as they went along with her.

Chapter Five

obby and his mate chose the tall elm in the front yard for their second nest of the season. It was a very hot summer and there was more breeze high up in the tree. When the eggs hatched, Robby was kept busy gathering food for the hungry babies. But he often took time out to perch on his favorite branch and call to us. Many times he had a worm in his mouth, and we laughed and wondered how he could talk and not drop the worm. Maybe he wanted to make sure we knew he had a family to feed now. His mate had grown very talkative also. She was the one who made sure we knew when something was bothering her and her little family.

Robby was a very strict father. If his children did not do as he wished he would really sound off. One day he flew to the kitchen area very agitated. I went out to see what was wrong. By the way he was fluttering and calling I knew he had lost one of his babies and needed help. I began to search and soon found one little birdie on the ground, tucked in close to the back of the pump house. I picked up the little one and took it out where Robby was waiting. After showing him that I had it in my hand, I put it on the grass in front of him. He was so happy that his baby was all right. He flew over by it and took it to the blue spruce grove where the others were. This was in August.

When they were able to fly about, Robby delighted in taking them into the raspberry patch where they could help themselves to the juicy berries. Other birds fed there too, and when we went into the patch to pick, they'd make a big fuss. Robby never scolded us, but would fly out of the berry patch and wait for us to leave. He felt he was welcome to anything we had, so he was willing to wait his turn. When it became necessary to irrigate the garden, he stayed close by to get any worms that happened to come above the ground. He thought we were doing these things just for him. And he was happy when we cultivated the big berry patch—more worms. His mate was always close at hand to get her share, too, chirping and chattering just as Robby did.

By the last of October Robby, his mate, and their babies were ready to migrate with the rest of the flock. Before leaving, they came to us as a family to say goodbye.

Our bantams could be seen anyplace in the area close by the barn. The time was getting late for hens to steal a nest, but we had a little red hen that did just that. She found a nice secluded place and laid 14 eggs. The rooster that had fathered the future brood was the one we called Speckles. He was a beautiful bird—mostly white with many small, colored feathers sprinkled in his coat. The way he strutted, he must have felt he was very special too.

Everything went well until she hatched the eggs and took her 12 tiny babies out to forage for food. Speckles decided he did not want to be responsible for a bunch of "kids," so he left her stranded alone. The other banties noticed this, and they must have had their rules also, for they chased Speckles out of the barn at feeding time. He had to wait until the others had gone to roost before he was allowed in the barn.

Another little red rooster came to the new mother's aid, staying with her to help with her chicks. The weather was already getting quite cold, and the babies were still quite small. "Mom" and the red rooster would bring the little flock up to the kitchen porch for food. We'd see the little red rooster sitting by her side with some of the babies under him also. I heard two birds clucking to the babies and was surprised to find the little red rooster was clucking also.

Later, when the winter set in with a vengeance, the banties would not let Speckles eat with them. He was forced to come to the house when he got hungry enough to brave the snowdrifts. He would stay on the sidewalk by the porch, standing first on one foot and then the other because of the cold, and wait until we fed him. Poor Speckles. He was willing to eat corn from our hands, he was so hungry.

Our laying hens were snug in their own coop. We kept them very clean, as we could not tolerate eating eggs from hens that lived in a dirty house. Weekly, we scraped and cleaned their coop and gave them clean straw to scratch in. We kept two roosters with them. All of them were pets and never were afraid or upset when we came in to clean. I always came with a pocket full of corn and they knew it. When everything was clean I'd sit down by the feeder. Before long, I'd be surrounded by hens trying to get in my pocket.

The two roosters had their self-appointed jobs to do also. In the morning when the lights came on, one rooster stayed down below and made sure no hen stayed under the roost to catch another nap, while the other one went on top of the roost and chased the lazy ones down to eat. After all, if they did not eat, they would not lay eggs.

We had our own formula for a vegetarian egg mash, and the hens thrived on it. The eggs actually had a better flavor, and we never lacked for customers. Feeding them this special diet, we did not have sick chickens. It even made a difference in their dispositions, for they were much quieter than the usual flock that was fed mash made with meat scraps.

Chapter Six

When spring came we again waited for Robby to arrive. He flew in with a flock of robins on March 14, 1971. He had time to play around with the others during the first two weeks, so we didn't see much of him until his mate arrived.

We'd put up a heavy wire trellis by the front porch for the ivy vines to climb. At the top the wires had bent over making a little shelf about 14 inches from the trellis top and under the roof of the porch. This is where Robby and his mate decided to make their first nest. It was a secluded place, safe from the wind and rain. All was well until their eggs were laid, then something got in and destroyed them all. They deserted the nest, and we wondered what they would do next.

One morning as I went outside, Robby met me with a long piece of straw in his beak. He called to me and flew up into the tall elm in the backyard. He kept calling me, so I watched to see what he had on his mind. He flew up into the tree and landed on a branch where a cluster of small branches came together—a perfect place to build a nest. Then he took the straw that he had in his beak and kept turning around and around as if to say he would be making a nest there. When I told my husband what Robby was trying to tell me, he just looked at me and laughed as if to say that I had a good imagination.

About 10:00 he came into the kitchen and said, "You can't guess what Robby is doing."

We went outside and there in that exact spot Robby had told me about, he and his mate had built a very nice nest. They had found a good puddle of water near the garden, making it convenient to take mud up to secure the straw and other materials for their nest.

A large spring-fed irrigation pond had been dug about two blocks east of our farmyard. Hidden on the west side of the pond we found a nest of pheasant eggs. She thought she had chosen a secluded spot where her nest would not be found, and we didn't disturb it. Just beyond the pond lay a wooded area left in its natural state for the birds and animals that wished to live there.

While preparing a field just beyond this area for planting, Tom noticed a family of foxes watching him work. The little foxes were very curious and would come out to watch when he was far away, hiding when he came near. We had drainage ditches on two sides of the acreage, and during two different years a family of beavers made a dam there. We had to have the game warden come out to move them to another area so our ditch would not overflow.

Robby and his mate were doing fine. They had nestlings now and were busy carrying worms to their hungry mouths. One day I heard Robby calling from the top of our shop. I hurried out to discover his problem and saw several grackles in his tree. He apparently felt he couldn't cope with so many birds so called for help. I got the gun and shot up in the air, and that satisfied him. The grackles flew away, and he felt his family was safe. Unfortunately, we found robin eggs lying in the yard so figured the grackles had robbed another bird's nest.

I found another pheasant's nest with 19 eggs in it. The mother was sitting on it. Sadly, a few days later I discovered that an animal had killed the mother, and most of her eggs were broken and destroyed. The eggs would have hatched in a few days. Sometimes nature reminds us that sin is still in our world.

The martins arrived on May 18th, but had a rough time keeping the sparrows away. The sparrows wanted their house and were willing to fight for it.

The barn swallows were busy also. They'd built their nests inside the barn near the very top, but the sparrows were not interested in them.

One day Tom and I were down by the irrigation pond when Robby discovered us there. He had been busy feeding babies all week, but he was not too busy to visit and sing to us.

In the evenings Robby liked to be with us and would follow us wherever we went. He would sing and talk to us and expect us to talk to him, too. Often Tom whistled to him, and he liked that. When he was satisfied knowing what we were doing, Robby would go back to the house and stay with his mate and family for the night. He and his mate kept busy during the day, gathering worms for their hungry babies.

When they saw a cat nearby is when *she* would call us for help. She had a certain cat call, and she knew we'd come to help her. If we couldn't see the cat, she would follow it, and we would follow her. By this time she knew we were her friends.

When the baby robins left the nest, their parents watched them closely because the grackles were nearby and ready to torment them. One day a baby flew out of the nest and landed on Tom's shoulder. He peeped and peeped, then flew into the lilacs. It was fun to see the little ones—with their short tails—trying to fly, and to see the parents watching them so closely.

One day at about 3:00 p.m., we saw the sky getting dark. It looked just like a dark, deep wave of water coming to engulf us. The air felt cold and icy, as if it might bring hail. When the storm struck, the wind was strong and the rain came down in heavy blasts. Tom was out cutting asparagus before the storm struck and heard Robby give warnings to his babies, as if to say, "Danger, find shelter!"

The next day Robby was singing again

at daybreak, so apparently all was well with his family. We looked up at his nest and found it was still snug and tight where they had built it, even though they were not using it now. We were still finding robin eggs on the lawn, so we knew the nest robbers were still at work.

Chapter Seven

One day as I was walking in the blue spruce grove, I found a pheasant's nest. Looking more closely, I saw that a bantam hen had laid two eggs in the nest next to the others. I knew if the bantam eggs hatched, the tiny babies could not keep up with the fast moving pheasants. So I went to the house for a spoon and reached carefully into the nest to remove the two small eggs. I took them to the house and put them under a light to see if they would hatch.

The next day I was checking to see if they were all right when I noticed one egg had already "pipped." I stayed there and watched the little one break the egg shell and come out. Tom walked into the kitchen just then and asked what I would do with it. I said I would take care of it myself. He laughed and wondered how that would turn out. The second egg didn't hatch, so I just had the one very tiny little black chick. Now to take care of it with my busy schedule!

The only thing I had to feed the chick was oatmeal, so I got that ready. I tapped my finger on the food for the bantam, and it got the message. At night it was content to sleep in a shoebox under a feather duster. Later I moved it to a cardboard box with a screen over the top. An electric light above it was enough to keep it warm. I got some cracked grain to feed it, and it grew quickly and became very tame.

When the weather was warm enough, I fixed a small fenced area nearby so it would be safe by itself. When Tom and I sat in the yard in the evening, it was not content to stay in its little pen, so I would let it out. It wasn't long before it hopped to our shoulders or onto our laps. We could see it was a little hen, but such a tiny one. We called her Little Peep.

When we found a weak baby chick among the group of banties I took it indoors to hand feed it and try to keep it alive. But

43

we almost gave up on this baby chick, for we just couldn't get it to eat or drink except with an eye-dropper. Then we had an idea. We took it outside and put it in the pen with Little Peep. The chick began to follow Little Peep around, which gave it good exercise and maybe made it hungry, for it would eat when Little Peep ate. By nightfall, it was so exhausted it was satisfied to sleep under the feather duster near its larger friend.

When Little Peep was old enough to be let out of her yard, she would follow us wherever she could. She would not have a thing to do with the other banties; she thought she was a person. She was happy to come into the kitchen at night and jump into her box—she knew this was her place. She was even willing to share it with the other little chick.

As Little Peep grew older, she wanted to go around the house and roost in the lilac tree. We were afraid for her safety so we took her inside for the night. Later, when she was old enough, we took her out to the chicken coop.

The white hens did not want a little black chicken to invade their coop, so she had a difficult time. Thankfully, she was so fast that she had no trouble escaping their beaks. She'd run under the roost where it was dark and her color helped her to hide. At night she roosted on the electric wires above. She was so small she could get by with it. In time, the hens allowed her to be there and seemed to accept her.

As Little Peep grew older, I wondered if she would begin to lay eggs. She was always friendly and when I went into the coop would fly up on my shoulder. Then one day she flew up to my shoulder, then over to the nesting box on the wall, and then back to my shoulder. I went over to look in the nest, and there was the tiniest little egg. She was so proud of it and wanted me to see what she had done. She continued to lay and was content to stay in the coop with the other hens.

On July 4 we heard Robby calling and tried to find him. His chirp sounded so far away, but we finally saw him nearby on his favorite dead branch in the elm. His beak was full of nesting material. That's why his voice was so low—he couldn't open his beak wide to call us. When he saw we'd caught his eye, he flew up into the same tree and started to arrange the material on a new branch with small twigs just like he'd done with his last nest. This one was closer to the ground and in a place where we could watch what was going on.

The starlings were not around, and Robby hoped to have the tree without any disturbance. Just as before, he wanted to get my attention so I'd know where he was building. I made sure there was a puddle of water handy so he'd have mud for "gluing" the twigs and grass together. After his building session, he went over and took a dip in the puddle, and then flew up on the clothesline pole to preen and fluff his feathers. He had no objections to our watching him. After this, he and his mate had a good time frolicking in the tree and garden area.

A few days later Robby called me with some news to tell. He flew up to his nest, and his mate flew out to the cornfield to feed. He flew back to his favorite bare branch and talked just a bit before flying back to his nest. He was trying to tell me they were now beginning to set on the new batch of eggs, and he was taking his turn. He had been having his evening chats regularly and singing before daybreak, so we knew they were serious about their homemaking.

They hatched only a couple of babies this time, so didn't have much work to do gathering worms. They had more time to play and visit with us. He liked to sit on the branch with a big worm in his mouth and visit at the same time. Both birds were very friendly. But when the babies left the nest, they spent more time caring for them and less time visiting with us.

Now they were busy getting ready for the long trip south. Their feathers were molting and sometimes Robby looked really rugged. We'd hear him early in the mornings or late evenings from the pasture trees. At times, he'd sit close by and sing to us, but this was their time to relax and have fun, with no babies to protect and care for.

We heard Robby call one morning, so we knew he was still around. But he called softly, so it was hard to locate him where he sat on the dead limb of the plum tree. He talked for a minute and flew away to our larger greenhouse. We'd had company earlier in the day and were sitting on the porch when we saw Robby walking on the nearby picnic table, watching us. He didn't reply to our talking to him but listened to every word. He seemed to get some satisfaction just being near and being a part of the family.

It was very dry and worms were not easily found, but he seemed to be getting enough to eat. There were only a few robins in our area, but Robby had stayed very close by us this year.

One morning Robby and his mate came near the house. Tom whistled to him and had a bit of conversation. This satisfied them and they both flew away. That was October 23. We saw them no more, so we knew they had gone south for the winter.

Chapter Eight

It had been a very cold winter with a lot of snow, but it was now time for the robins to return. We were eager to see them. And on March 20, 1972, at 6:00 p.m., Robby flew in with a few other robins. He could see me through the window and began calling, so I went outside to greet him. He had flown down to a tree in the pasture. But when I called to him, he flew back to his favorite branch—where he knew I could see him—and burst into song. It was already getting a bit dark, so I was surprised that he was so interested in greeting me. But "hellos" can't wait when one has been away so long. Soon it began to rain, so he flew off to find shelter for the night.

The next few days were damp, cool, and cloudy, with a brisk wind. He didn't return for another week. Then early one morning he came and called his cheery "hello." It promised to be a lovely day, but by evening the weather changed and it was spitting snow. The temperature was near freezing.

We didn't see him very often, for this was his time to play around. He was very friendly, but independent. His visits were brief, as if he had a lot to do before having to settle down to raise a family.

The weather had been cold and rainy, so we did not notice the return of the females until April 12. When the mornings were bright and sunny, the birds would fill the air with song. It was a joy to wake up.

After the arrival of his mate, Robby began his usual pattern of friendliness. When he wished to talk, he was persistent and called us repeatedly until we came to visit with him. When we called to him, sometimes other robins answered. We could always tell which one was Robby by the way he squatted and flipped his tail. He still had the habit he had begun when I hand-fed him as a baby.

We knew it was near nesting time, so we made sure there was always a puddle of water nearby for them to use when building their nest. We saved strings and lint from the dryer for them if they wanted to add it to their nest too. They always used the things we put out for them.

For their first nest, they chose the place among the ivy vines just under the front porch roof. They still thought this was a good place, even if it had been robbed the year before. They built another layer of sticks and grass and mud on top of their old nest. This really surprised me, but they raised this nest of babies successfully.

One evening some friends came to visit us to get a pair of bantams to take home with them. The man was a herdsman on a large dairy farm and knew of places where bantams could live undisturbed. We thought it would be a good home for Speckles, where he could be king. They could choose a little hen to go with him, too.

While we were in the living room visiting with them, Robby came to the picture window and called for me. I knew he wouldn't come by so late if he wasn't having trouble. Tom said I should ignore him, but I was sure he needed help. The lady visiting us said she wanted to see what was happening, so when I left the room, she followed. As I passed through the kitchen, I reached in a drawer for a flashlight. I could see that Robby, who was always a good window peeper, had followed me around the house and was waiting for me by the kitchen door.

I followed him out into the grove of trees where all the robins roosted. All the other birds were upset too, and I knew they must have a big problem they could not handle by themselves. As I walked into the grove, I saw a large owl fly out of a tree and across the road into the grove of trees on the neighbor's farm.

The birds stopped fussing, and I heard a flurry of wings as they all flew back into the grove. That's why Robby came to me for help. Now that the owl had flown away, Robby flew up to the top of the greenhouse and sang a full song for me. It was almost dark, so I knew it was his way of saying thank you. Now all was quiet, and I heard no more from Robby or the other birds that night.

We were waiting for it to get dark so we could go to the barn and pick up Speckles from the bantams' roosting place. Then our friends could take him and choose a hen to take with him.

We visited them a few weeks later, and they took us out to see the bantams.

Speckles and his mate were both very happy in their new home. They had a large room all to themselves.

Chapter Nine

For their next nest, Robby and his mate went into the blue spruce grove, building their nest about five feet from the ground. When Robby led me out there, three beautiful blue eggs already lay in the nest and his mate was busy keeping them warm. By this time she was no longer afraid of me, and I crept slowly up to her, talking quietly as I came closer. I kept my hands down and made no move to touch her. I stopped two feet from her and she didn't move a feather, but her eyes were glued to me.

Later I was telling my neighbor, Phyllis, about it, and she said she wanted to see the nest, too. I told her she couldn't do it.

"If you can do it, I can do it," she said, and wanted to try. She walked slowly toward the nest. But when she got about 15 feet away, Robby swooped down and "buzzed" her head. He had been guarding his mate and their nest from the top of a nearby elm.

Phyllis hurried back to me and agreed that Robby would not let her go near his mate. Robby knew he had to watch carefully, as grackles were all around. He didn't want to lose this nest of eggs.

When the eggs hatched, Robby and his mate tenderly cared for the babies without any problem.

We had a big white hen that wanted to set, so we gave her a setting of eggs and a little house all by herself. A few days after she hatched her little chicks, we moved her little house near the pump house so I could keep an eye on her.

One morning at 4:00 a.m. we were awakened by her screams. We both dashed out to see what her problem was and found she had been frightened by an animal that had killed all her chicks. She had tipped her little house over and was in the yard making a terrible noise, as only a hen can do. Tom gathered up her dead babies and moved the house to another place, while I picked up my pet hen and tried to calm her down. After a few minutes, she was quiet so we could leave her.

Tom asked me what I planned to do with her, now that her chicks were dead. I told him I would be at the door of the hatchery in the next town when they opened their door in the morning. I was able to get a dozen chicks, and when I returned I knelt down to give the babies to her. When I handed her the first chick, she clucked and pushed it under her body. She did the same with each one, but the last chick just stood there and squawked. The mother hen reached over and gave him a good whack on the bottom. He was glad to scoot underneath her.

She had the freedom of the farmyard until her little ones began to crow. It was good to hear them give their first squeaky crow. Then a customer bought all her chicks, and she returned to the chicken coop.

Two years earlier we had planted a row of small pine trees next to the driveway. I noticed some activity among these little trees, and I found that chipping sparrows were building their nests there. We watched as they built their tiny nests, laid their eggs, and raised their little ones close by.

One day my daughter came to visit us and brought us a big, beautiful yellow cat. It had been owned by someone who had spent a lot of time training it. We knew it was a house cat and had to be kept indoors at night. We also found it had been toilet trained. If a board with a hole in it was placed on the toilet seat, the cat did not need a litter box. It liked to be rocked and would lay in my arms like a baby as long as I would take the time to do it.

The only problem it had was that it liked to catch birds. That was a *big* problem. I put a bell around its neck, but it knew how to keep it from ringing and soon found a nest of indigo buntings. It ate all but the head of one and brought the head and laid it at my husband's feet. Poor kitty. It didn't know it had committed a crime. But that was the end of that cat's welcome with us!

One of my neighbors badly wanted the cat. I called her and told her if she came before I changed my mind, she could have it. Needless to say, she came over as soon as she could. I had told her the cat would knock on the kitchen door when it wanted to come into the house, but she wouldn't believe me. After she got the cat, they watched from a distance just to see if I was telling the truth. The cat really did knock on the door, and they treated it like royalty after that.

Robby and his mate finished their last nesting early. We thought they might make a third nest, but they weren't interested. They took their own sweet time raising these babies and had plenty of time just to play around.

Robby shared bits of bird news with us. When molting time came we knew he was around but didn't feel much like talking. On September 23 he flew in with a few robins and called with his old zestful nature. He would talk with us a bit and then fly off to join the other robins. We could see that he and his mate were both full-feathered now. He was as friendly as ever, but more independent, and would swoop over our heads as he flew across the yard. We missed his persistent conversations. His habits changed every year, and now it seemed that he didn't need our company as he had in the past.

On October 12 I went over to see a friend. While I was there, Robby came over and called from the tree in her yard. He made certain I knew he was there, for he had something to tell me. He was saying goodbye and wanted to be sure I knew. Three days later it began to snow—big, wet flakes. Apparently Robby knew this was coming and wanted to leave before it happened.

Chapter Ten

On March 12, 1973, Robby came back during the night on a strong south wind. He was waiting with his cheery greeting when Tom went out to begin work early in the morning. He must have been waiting for some time, for he didn't talk too long. He just wanted us to know he had returned, and soon went on his way. He came back to see us the next morning and spent more time filling us in on his trip south and back.

He came back each day to chat a bit and was very responsive—more than in other years before his mate had arrived. If he was within hearing distance he answered when we called his name.

Robby discovered the compost pile and found that he could get an easy meal of earthworms without much work. We'd had quite a bit of rain, which helped soften the ground. Robby still had all his old habits. He remembered his favorite trees and perching places, and he still gave us the warning of coming rain.

In the evenings we saw many other young robins and heard their chirping, but we could always tell which one was Robby because of the way he flipped his wings and tail. He had not forgotten that, even though he was almost 4 years old.

It was still early April and Robby and his mate were in no hurry to make a nest. They stayed closer to us and seemed to be curious about what we were doing. We were very busy in our greenhouses this time of year, and they liked to watch us work. When we sat in the living room in the evenings, Robby would sit in the big tree just outside and watch us through the window. He still remembered when he lived inside with us. When he called to us, I'd go to the door and let him know I heard him. That always made him happy.

We wondered when Robby and his mate would start their first nest. Perhaps they were slow because it had been very cold. We were watching to see if they would claim the front porch among the ivy vines.

We heard a lot of commotion on the front porch and found a grackle had built a nest right beside Robby's old one. I took it away, hoping to discourage the grackles and make less problems for Robby. Apparently Robby claimed that area for his partner and himself and was willing to chase the offenders out.

On April 29 we saw his mate carrying material for her nest. Robby was stationed in a nearby bush. When he wasn't helping her, he watched closely to see that she had no problems. We thought they would build another story on their old nest, but they didn't. They built another nest right beside the one from last year.

We could see why they had chosen that particular place, as our spring was so windy and rainy. They were able to hatch their babies without difficulty, but when the time came for Robby to baby-sit, he had a problem keeping them under control.

One evening after dark I grew afraid it would rain during the night, so I went out to shut the door of the chicken coop. During the day we left a screen door open so the chickens could have fresh air and sunshine in the coop. On my way back to the house, I heard a bird fall from a branch of the apple tree. My cocker dog bounded toward it, but I called her off and went over to see what it was. It was one of Robby's babies that had lost its grip on the branch. I picked it up and tried to get it back on the branch, but I could not, so I took it into the house for the night.

I found a cardboard box and stuck a wooden spoon into its sides for a roost, and the baby bird was content to stay there. Before dawn Robby must have counted his family and found one missing, for what a fuss he made! His cries woke me up, so I took his baby outside. I called to him and gave him his child. He was such a happy father. As for me, my sleep was ended, and my day had begun.

We noticed a pair of flickers had built a nest in a hole in the big elm over the kitchen porch. Their babies were almost ready to leave the nest, for we could see them hanging out the hole. The starlings had been a big nuisance and were giving these little ones a bad time. I wondered where the mother was, but I did not see her nearby to protect them. Then I noticed two nestlings had fallen out of the tree and were on the ground.

I picked them up to see if they were still alive. One had died, but the other one was frisky as could be. Now what was I to do with it?

This little flicker was happy, whatever I did. During the day I'd take it outside, and we'd go for a walk. I'd turn over all the rocks I saw along the way. The baby flicker knew what to do, diving in and eating any ant, ant egg, or any other edible thing it found. Before long I had another little friend that either sat on my shoulder or ran beside me.

In a few days it had grown big enough that I could put it on the edge of the tree trunk, and it would climb up the tree and hunt for food. At the end of the day I would call to it, and it would come down for the night. We called it Whitsey, as that is what its call sounded like to us. We knew it would soon be able to find food and shelter for itself.

We had decided to sell the farm and move to the south, where the winters were not so severe. So we stored the things that we did not sell and started out to find a place that would be ideal for Tom's health. When we returned, we began to load the big

U-Haul. Robby could tell something was happening that he could not understand.

Robby and his mate had built their nest in the large elm in the backyard, and the mother bird was setting on her eggs. Robby was distressed as he watched us take furniture from the house, but we could not tell him what was going on.

By the time we finished packing, the people who had bought our farm had already moved in, so we moved the big truck and our cars over to Phyllis' house. We planned to leave at 3:00 in the morning, as we knew Robby would follow us if we did not leave very early.

Phyllis told us later that Robby was very disturbed when he found we had gotten away without his knowing it. He had come up to their place and called and called. He knew her well and came there often to talk to her.

When we left our home and farm, we thought we would never see Robby again. We felt badly, as he was a big part of our lives. We knew he could survive without us, but we would miss him.

We enjoyed the mild winter at our new home in North Carolina. Both Tom and I had gotten work and were happy there. On the morning of February 28, 1974, I was on the deck putting feed out for the birds when I thought I heard a familiar call. It sounded like Robby, but I could not believe my ears. Still, I answered the call in the same way I'd always answered Robby in the past.

I went indoors to tell Tom about it, and, like me, he couldn't believe it. We were in a hurry to get to work, so we gave it no more thought.

Tom got home from work before I did and found a robin waiting in the flowering cherry tree right above where Tom parked his car. The robin visited with Tom, chattering and talking as Robby always did. Tom was convinced it was Robby, even though it seemed impossible.

We realized that Robby had seen both of our cars parked side by side as they always were when we lived on the farm, so Tom was sure he had found us. We discovered later that the robins' migration path to the north came across this area.

Robby seemed to be confused as to why we were here instead of back in Minnesota, but seemed overjoyed to find us. He had many things to tell us, and each day he spent a lot of time near us, singing his sweet songs. He apparently had spent his winter in a place where he could find good food, as he looked so fat and finely feathered.

In the morning of March 7 Robby called to me, and I went out on the deck to see what he wanted. He was sitting on a nearby limb, preening his feathers and showing me how big and beautiful he was. His color was vivid, and he seemed to be much brighter and more beautiful than the local robins.

He had something of great importance to tell me, for he talked and talked for half an hour, then jumped down and ate a big worm he found under the pine tree. He seemed to like what he was finding here. During this time Robby would get very close to us. Often there were other robins around that drew his attention, so I'd leave them to their bird business. We were getting used to waking up in the mornings listening to his beautiful song. When we worked outside, it was a pleasure to have him near. We thought he would soon be leaving for Minnesota, but we looked forward to his trip next year, and hoped he would visit us again now that he knew where we were.

Chapter Eleven

Robby wasn't around for the next three days, and we missed him. We didn't know he had gone to get his mate and bring her back with him.

On March 11 I went out the front door to get the mail, when a robin swooped by me and called. I called back. I could see it was a female by its coloring. I thought that she looked and sounded like Robby's mate, but figured I was just imagining it. So I went indoors and continued my work.

A few minutes later I went out the back door, only to find both Robby and his mate feeding on worms just about 10 feet from the patio. When they saw me, they both lifted their heads and called, as if to say "We are both here to stay."

They had returned during the night. She had been trying to let me know she had arrived and was glad to be with us. She was very tame and let us get close to her.

They had made themselves right at home. When my husband tilled in the garden, they kept close by to get the big, fat worms. As before, when it was dry, Tom turned on the irrigation. They knew the water made the ground soft, so they could easily get their fill of worms.

One morning we saw them both carrying nesting material into a young pine tree. But when they saw that we had noticed, they dropped it and went on looking for worms. A few days later they went over to the neighbors' yard about 50 feet away and built their nest in the bush against their home.

The morning after the nest was finished, they showed us where they had built it. By May 1 she was setting on her eggs. The blue jays were a nuisance, and Robby kept busy chasing them away. We noticed that the native robins were ahead of our two, already feeding their little ones. One robin got a big worm and chopped it up in 2-inch pieces. He took two or three pieces at a time to his babies. His nest was across the creek.

The hummingbirds were busy feeding from the syrup feeder, and the chickadees, titmouse, towhees, goldfinches, and cardinals were coming to the seed feeder also. The blue jays and grackles were still a nuisance.

Robby's mate made it her job to tell me when a cat was near. She would follow the cat and call to me so I could bring the gun, even if it was not loaded, to chase it away. She remembered that from the farm. She would follow the cat until it crossed the creek where it lived. Robby was very quiet, but he always kept a close watch on his new home.

His habits seemed to change every year, but he was just as possessive of us as ever. He was used to our large farm in Minnesota, so had chosen the neighbor's yard as part of his hunting space. The neighbors seemed to enjoy them as much as we did.

We knew when the babies hatched, as they let us see them carrying worms to feed them. Two weeks after hatching, the babies left their nest, and Robby's big job began. Other birds had half-grown babies too, and they all had big problems with the cats across the creek. I'm sure the cats ate quite a few baby birds.

The feeding job had not been a big chore for the birds, as we did not see them working as hard as in other years. They had more time to play around, but they always managed to keep an eye on us and watch what we were doing. One day we were planting tomatoes, and Robby sat in a nearby tree watching everything we did.

When we drove away, he would follow us. We wondered if he was afraid we would leave him again.

They began their second nest on June 21 in the big pine tree between our home and the neighbor's. The babies hatched on July 5 and were out of the nest by July 19. Robby was baby-sitting again and let his mate do most of the talking to us this time. His habits seemed to change again, and he watched quietly, but did not miss a thing.

One October day we decided to drive a few miles out to an apple orchard. We gave no thought to the birds, but soon we heard Robby singing. He had followed us and was sitting on a wire above our heads, watching us pick apples. He wanted to let us know he was there.

When we went visiting our friends, he would follow and let us know he was there also. It seemed to make him happy for us to know he was near.

Robby and his mate left for migration on November 18th. But before they left, they brought their whole family—from the two nests—up close to the back patio. They'd never brought all their babies so close to us before, so we knew it was to say goodbye.

Our winters were so very mild compared to what we were used to in Minnesota. We did have a snowfall or two, but it melted in about 48 hours, and we thought that was great.

Robby returned for the first time on January 10, 1975, and stayed just two days. He called from the creek, where he perched high up in a tall tree. His mate and his last year's family were with him. We walked down where they were and talked to them and then they were satisfied. We wondered if they had come back to see for sure if we were still where they left us. Robby sang his spring song for us, but the next two days were rainy and cold, so he flew away.

He and his mate came back on January 26. They brought their family, and we saw them in the backyard pulling worms. They were still checking the neighbor's backyard for worms, for they had been made to feel welcome there also.

It was a pleasure to watch them while they were on the ground feeding. They did not talk much at that time, as they seemed to be listening, and then would jump in for the worm. Robby's spring song was beautiful and so very clear, and we were always willing to listen.

After a good day of feeding and playing around, Robby faithfully came up to sing his good-night song before going off to roost. He and his little wife seemed to be later with their nesting plans than the native birds.

Then we were away for about ten days, so we were not home when they came to say good night. When we returned, they did not come in the evenings for a few days, but when they found us there, they began their old evening habit again.

One day Tom decided to till the garden to get it ready for spring planting. Robby watched from a nearby bush, then flew back to the house. I was busy in the kitchen, but heard him calling from the deck. I went to see what he wanted, and he flew toward the garden, calling to me as he flew. He wanted me to know that Tom was working up the soil to make it easier for him to get the worms, and he really appreciated it, as it was beginning to get a bit dry.

We noticed they were flying in and out of the bush by the neighbor's house, and we could tell they were thinking of making their next nest there. We saw that the female watched closely whenever a cat came around and would give her shrill cat call so I could chase it away. We were surprised they were interested in making a nest now, as it was early in April, a whole month earlier than when they built in Minnesota.

Then Tom turned on the irrigation to water the freshly planted strawberry plants. Of course, Robby thought he turned it on just to make it easier for him to get worms.

They made their nest in the bush. She laid her eggs and began to set in earnest. Each morning before I went to work, I would go over to see her. She would sit very tight and watch me, but not move. Robby was nearby watching, but was not afraid.

The eggs hatched on April 20. We kept watering the strawberry plants, which made it easier for them to find food for the babies. When their babies were about a week old, something messed up their nest and the babies were missing. We did not know what happened, but it was a very sad, frightening thing for both of the birds.

So we were really surprised when they

built their next nest in the very same bush. They began to lay eggs on May 13. About a week later we were more surprised to find that something had gotten into their nest and had broken all the eggs and ruined the nest. Both of the birds were feeling bad, and Robby seemed to be reverting back to his old baby habits. We watched to see if his mate was doing all right, as it must have been very difficult for her, too.

Robby did not come near to visit for several days. Finally he came close, and we felt their mourning time was over. Now he was coming closer, was continually watching, and was very attentive as in times past. He came with us when we worked in the garden and sang constantly during the day and evening. We wondered why he did not get a sore throat, or at least get tired, but he did not. His mate was always near to us and would talk to us if she could get a word in between his songs.

A few days passed. We were afraid something had happened to Robby's mate, as we did not see her around as usual. One evening we decided to visit friends a mile or so away. Several of us gathered in the screened-in area of their home. In just a few minutes Robby and his mate came up beside the area, sat on a bush, and began talking to us. Our friends knew about Robby and his mate, but now they experienced Robby's personal interest in us. We were favored with a serenade, which we all enjoyed.

At times, Robby would perch on a high limb of a tree and call from there. He was not satisfied until he was able to catch our eye, and then he would fly away. His eyes were a lot sharper than ours.

He'd become acquainted with some of our friends whom we sometimes visited, and he'd fly over to see them by himself. They would recognize him by his insistent calling and go out to talk to him. Then he was satisfied and would fly away.

One day we decided to go to a camp meeting about 25 miles away, not giving much thought to Robby and his mate. When we arrived there, we parked the car and walked to the auditorium. We could hardly believe our eyes when Robby met us and gave us his familiar call and burst into song.

He flew up to a branch just outside the entry door and stayed there while we were inside, singing most of the time. It was late in the day when we came outside, planning to leave and get home before dark. Just as we were leaving the area for the parking lot,

Robby swooped down in front of us and gave us his good-night call. He got home first and was waiting in a tree by the side of the house. He gave us his greeting, just as if to let us know he'd arrived ahead of us. He then flew off to his roost for the night.

He followed us to camp meeting one more time, and on the third evening he was right there to see if we were going again When he saw us leave in separate cars, he thought we were going to work as usual, but he flew up in a pine tree and watched to make sure. When we went back for church that weekend, he followed us again. What a bird!

We always set posts in the garden for trellising so that the beans, tomatoes, and cucumbers would have a place to climb. We stretched a wire along the top of the posts and another lower down, and put strings between the wires for the vegetables to climb on. Robby really liked this, as it gave him more places to sit when he visited us while we worked.

We noticed that a dove had built its nest in among the grapes. She was satisfied with a flimsy nest, and had laid only one egg in it so far.

Soon the strawberries began to ripen, and Robby was willing to share with us. Bob whites, cardinals, brown thrashers, and other birds came in from the trees by the creek to enjoy the berries, too. While picking the berries, we noticed the song sparrows had built their nests among the plants, and we tried to protect them. The mothers seemed to enjoy being near us while the young ones picked bugs among the plants.

Robby seemed to know about what time we got up in the morning and felt we should wake up to music. When he was sure we were up and about, he would go on his merry way. It seemed right after a rain he had more time for singing, as he got his fill of worms more quickly.

Whenever we took vegetables from the garden, he was nearby to watch what we were doing. He seemed to be interested in everything we did.

We discovered they were following us when we went to church. One of the windows was open and we could hear Robby singing. We were sitting close by, so he could see us from the outside.

It was time for nesting again, but this time they went to the opposite side of the neighbor's house, hoping to get away from whatever had been destroying their nest. But this nest was destroyed also. For the next they went across the creek in the high trees. From this nest they raised three babies without problems.

We had a fuchsia plant hanging on the deck, and we noticed a Carolina wren building her nest there. She built a covered house of soft weeds and lined it with soft material, leaving just a hole to enter and leave. We tried to water the plant so it would not hurt the wrens, but they had damaged the roots of the plant so much that it died.

During molting time Robby and his mate became very quiet and listless. They would sit motionless in a tree and talk very low— almost too low to be heard, as if they had very little energy. But they were near enough to see what we were doing. As their feathers became full and smooth, they became more active and loud.

Robby still liked to sit very high in the trees and call to us. When we could not see him, he would fly to another place so we could see him move. Then he would be satisfied. Many times he would swoop over our heads and call to us, but was too busy to stop. When they felt they wanted to chat, they would insist that we take time out to visit. When they were finished, they would fly away.

We decided to get a different car and wondered how they would react to that. For a few days they were perplexed, but soon they realized what had happened. They followed me around to make sure it was my car.

About this time, I decided to fly to the West Coast to visit my father. My husband did not go, so the birds wondered what had happened to me. I returned on November 7. The next morning when we arrived at church, there was Robby's mate waiting for me by the parking lot. She made sure we knew she was there and seemed happy to know that I had returned home again. After filling me in on all the news I had missed, she was satisfied to go join her family, as they had already left for the Southland.

Chapter Twelve

January 1, 1976, was a lovely day. We were not expecting our robin friends so soon, but Tom called me outside to see them. They were calling to us from a tall tree across the creek. We walked toward them, and when we were almost down to the creek, Robby began to sing. They talked a bit and were satisfied that we knew they were back. We didn't stay long, for the ground was wet from the ice and snow that had fallen the previous week.

They stayed in the tree talking to Tom as he worked in the yard behind the house doing odd jobs that had to be done. They only stayed one day this time, and we were glad they were gone, for the weather changed again for the worse.

They returned on February 2 to stay. They made sure we knew they were there, and watched Tom as he worked. The weather was unpredictable so early in the spring, so they only came on sunny days and found shelter on bad days.

As the good weather came, Robby was back to his old habits. We were awakened by his spring warbling. When he saw the bathroom lights go on, he knew we had gotten up. We would go out and call to him, and he was satisfied and would fly away.

One day we decided to take a walk with friends, and Robby and his mate went right along with us. He would call, and we would answer, so he knew we were aware of his presence.

An acquaintance who knew much about birds insisted that robins change mates every year. We knew that this wasn't true for Robby. But things were soon to change in Robby's life.

One day Robby's little mate was missing. We noticed that Robby had a wound on his breast that crossed from the upper left to the right side. He did not come around much for a few days, seemingly waiting for his sore breast to heal. The scar was noticeable, especially if he was wet. We could not know what had happened, as we could not understand what he tried to tell us. But we guessed that his mate had been caught by a cat, and he had been injured trying to save her, almost getting killed himself.

He did find a young female by April. They decided to build their nest in the hemlock tree by our front door. She didn't know us and did not approve of his being on such friendly terms. We mowed the front lawn, which made it easy for them to find bugs and worms. We were not getting as much rain as usual, so food was not as easily found. Robby made sure we were aware of their nest, but his new mate made quite a fuss when we came near. When Tom worked in the garden, Robby watched closely so he wouldn't miss any worms that were available.

When the babies hatched, we knew they would have a problem getting enough food for the little ones. One day I decided to dig worms for the mother, but the problem was to get her to accept them. I found a pan with sides just high enough so the worms would not crawl out before she could get them. I put the pan on the walk about 10 feet from her nest. Then I went indoors and watched from the window.

She soon found the pan. It was comical to see her circle the pan several times to size it up and decide if she dared to get in the pan for the worms she could see wiggling around. She jumped in and grabbed at one. Then she got a bit bolder and took one out on the walk, cut it up into pieces, and took a mouthful to her hungry babies. After she had fed them all, she waited for half an hour, keeping her babies warm, before repeating the process. When the pan was empty, I tried to get it so I could put more worms in it, but she wouldn't let me take it without a fuss. So I waited until after dark to get it. I hadn't realized they were so hungry. Robby did the best he could to feed his little ones.

When the babies left the nest, Robby brought them to the apple tree by the kitchen door so we could see them. I picked one up and told Robby what a fine baby he had. The mama flew up and let us know she did not want us so near her family. I placed the baby on a branch in the apple tree, and Robby took the little one and flew away. She let him know she was not interested in staying with him for the second nest. We figured we had just witnessed a divorce in birdland. She did not approve of his friendship with us.

There was no second nest for Robby this

season, so he spent much time just enjoying himself. Sometimes he would come up on the banister of the deck, look through the glass doors, and watch me do my work inside while he preened his feathers.

He stayed near us as we worked in the garden and would favor us with many songs and conversations. Sometimes he would try to talk with a berry in his mouth. He'd drop it, then fly down to get it.

Our deck was partially covered with wisteria vines, which he liked very much. Many times he would fly into the vines and serenade us from there. He was still watching over his little family and spending time with them.

By this time, I had acquired a good selection of red and yellow canaries. I stacked the cages on the wall where Robby could see them from the deck. He was very interested in them, but was not a bit jealous. After all, he knew he was the most important bird in our lives, as he'd also been a member of our household. It only gave him more to observe from the deck or the cherry tree, where he stationed himself so frequently.

Tom noticed that Robby followed him to work, about 10 miles one way. We realized we could not get by with anything. He watched so he could fly along beside our car when we neared home, as he used to do in Minnesota.

He went through the molt and was very quiet, spoke softly, and was not too active. We didn't know where he spent his winters, but we thought it was not too far away. He came back on December 31, and after that he chose the nice days to visit us until he came to stay for the season.

By March 5, 1977, he decided to set up a regular watch. He would sit in the pine tree by our bedroom window and begin to call. We decided we did not need an alarm clock with him around. If it was too windy, we missed his constant call and song, but we knew he was still watching.

One day I went to the mall to shop, and as I neared the entrance, I heard him call from the top of the building. He had followed me downtown. I did not answer him, but I caught his eye and waved my hand. He was satisfied and flew away. Tom said he was out following him around the rest of the day. We felt he had really gotten his exercise. He said an early good night and flew down to his roosting place for the night.

The female robins arrived on March 19. We'd wondered if he would be alone and have no nest or babies. But then we saw him fighting over a young female.

We were away for a few hours. When we came home, we found Robby's new mate building a nest among the wisteria vines on the deck railing. They didn't have mud on it yet, so Tom turned the water on so they could finish it. Robby tried to persuade his new wife that it was all right to be so near to us. Finally he sat in the nest for two days to prove it was safe. Then she was satisfied and willing to lay her eggs in it.

We decided to stay off the deck so we would not disturb her. She laid four eggs, but only three hatched. Food was plentiful, so they grew fast. It was a pleasure watching their devotion to their family. When she was out feeding, Robby would sit on the nest, keeping the little ones warm. When both parents were not on the nest, they were nearby keeping watch.

Robby had enjoyed having their nest on the deck. He would run back and forth on the deck rail and sometimes run on the deck floor. He seemed to delight in showing her he was not afraid. She accepted us to a degree, but was very quiet about it.

It was interesting to watch them coax the little ones out of the nest. The parents would wait below the nest with food, but refuse to bring it to them. Robby would constantly visit them, but take no food to them. When they were hungry enough, they would fly down to their parents to be fed. Then Robby's baby-sitting job would begin.

Chapter Thirteen

One day our grandson, Steve, who was working with a building crew, noticed a wild duck with several little ducklings trying to cross a well-traveled road. Cars were not stopping, and he knew the ducks would be killed. He and another person ran over to rescue them. They were able to save the mother and two of her babies, and he brought them to us, hoping they would be all right.

The mother duck and one baby died during the night, but the other little duckling seemed to be just fine. We fixed a pen for it and gave it a lot of tender, loving care. We knew that as soon as it was old enough, we would have to find it a permanent home where it could have water to swim in.

We decided to take it out to a park that was by a lake. We drove out one morning and found there were many ducks just like this one living in the lake. People took pleasure in feeding them, so they were very tame.

We placed the little one in the water among others just a bit older than this one. It seemed very pleased to be there among its own kind. We soon left, but returned the next day to see how it was getting along.

The little duck recognized us but was happy where it was. It had found a mother duck that was willing to adopt it, and followed closely behind her. When the mother would turn to the left, the baby would turn left, when she turned right, the baby turned right. We could see it was content to be with her and the rest of her brood. We were satisfied leaving it there.

For Robby's second nest they went across the creek, high up in one of the trees where it would be cooler during the hot summer days. We could not see what went on over there, but we knew everything was fine by the way they acted. Robby was still watching everything that went on in the garden and getting his share of berries. He watched to see when Tom cultivated so he could follow behind and pick up the worms that had been uncovered. He appreciated it when Tom irrigated the garden, making it easier to pull worms out of the soft soil.

In August they began to molt. They made themselves scarce a good share of the time. When they did appear, we noticed their tail feathers were different lengths and the head feathers had not all grown back yet. Robby acted as if he knew he was not good to be seen. They spent much time high up in the wild cherry tree with the other birds, eating the delicious fruit.

After the molt was finished, Robby came back to visit and sing as usual. He couldn't stay long, for he he had a lot to do before leaving for the winter.

The winter had been cold and stormy, with more snow than usual. We returned from Hawaii on January 9 and found the ground covered with four inches of ice and snow. What a change from the warm Hawaiian weather.

Robby returned on February 15, 1978. On March 2 we got seven inches of snow, and we could hear Robby calling from his shelter. The sun came out and the snow melted in a day or so, and Robby was again happy. His mate and last year's babies were also back. We noticed a mockingbird had arrived and claimed the territory, giving Robby a rough time.

One day the "mocker" was giving Robby a real bad time, and he came to Tom and begged for help. Tom had a broom in his hand, and when the bird took after Robby, Tom threw the broom at him. He missed him, of course, but it gave Robby courage and he started chasing him. The feathers flew from the "mocker" and after that they shared the area without problem.

Robby and his mate decided to build on the deck again. They made a second story on last year's nest among the wisteria vines. She laid five eggs and seemed content this year to accept us. When I would go out on the deck, she would sit still on her nest. We tried to give her as much privacy as possible, and she made no fuss.

When I knew she was out feeding, I would slip out with the camera and take pictures of the nest. Each day, I did that and got the nesting from beginning to end. One day I turned and found Robby sitting on the window sill just six feet away, watching me. He did not make a sound, and I knew he was not afraid. All five eggs hatched and the nest was really full. It kept them both busy feeding all those hungry mouths. All went well until the babies were almost ready to leave the nest.

In the morning I went out and peeked into the nest and was horrified to find only one baby there. What had gotten the other babies? I wondered where the parents were. They must know about the disaster, but they weren't feeding that little one. I went out looking for Robby.

As soon as I came outside, he met me by the apple tree. I felt so sorry for him. He was broken hearted and could not figure what had happened during the night. The night was warm, and they were not needed to keep the little ones covered. Something had gotten the babies while the parents were away.

He talked to me and his voice was filled with sorrow. I sympathized with him and tried to get him to feed the one that was left. He talked to me for sometime, but finally understood what he had to do and started feeding that last little one. We never did find out what happened to his family. They watched this last baby carefully. They knew we had not taken their babies so were willing to come to us for sympathy.

For their next nest, they went into the apple tree just about 15 feet from the deck. They had no problem this time and really enjoyed eating the apples that grew in the tree. They were close to the garden and the berry patch and also close to us and could visit while helping themselves to the food nearby. Robby and his present mate had been together for two years and I hoped nothing would happen to her.

Song sparrows nested in the bushes near the house. They had deserted one little baby, and I picked it up to take care of it. But it had a problem with its stomach and didn't live long.

Robby and his mate ate the wild cherries that grew down by the creek until their molt was completed. They were well fed. They left for the south on November 20.

They returned for a brief visit on December 6, but they must have known the winter was not over. After that we did not see them until January 13.

It began to rain, and with the falling temperature things were covered with ice. When the ice melted, Robby appeared and called to let us know he was back. We noted how fat and brightly colored he was. We looked around to see if he was alone, and saw his mate and his last year's family.

His mate appeared to have no objections to him visiting with us. I had trimmed the wisteria vines back quite a bit as they was taking over the whole deck. Robby and his mate weren't interested in nesting there this year. They chose to nest in the neighbor's rose bush. The babies hatched around May 7. We saw his mate carrying the egg shells away and bringing back worms. Robby would perch on the limb of the pine tree with a worm dangling from his beak and try to talk at the same time. At first the worms were small—for small tummies. We had three inches of rain and that meant we had to mow the grass which pleased them as it made it easier to find the bugs and worms. Then the strawberries began to ripen, and that made them happy.

Around the 25th he was baby-sitting again. There was a new cat in the neighborhood, and we heard Robby scolding and giving his babies emphatic instructions. We were afraid he might lose some of his babies to the cat, but they didn't and both stayed happy, going about their usual business.

A few days later we were awakened early by their distress calls right by our bedroom window. We looked where the birds perched on a branch and saw two huge cats crouching on the ground below, waiting hopefully for a good bird breakfast.

Tom put on his robe and went outside. As soon as the cats saw him, they ran for cover. Then the birds relaxed and settled down to their morning routine.

The mockingbird had accepted living in our backyard along with the robins. He awakened us at 5:00 a.m. with his many different songs. He found that near the berry patch was a good place to live, and he sang at the top of his voice, he was so happy. The other birds that nested in the trees by the creek also felt it was nice to be so close to such good food.

But the blue jays were giving all the different birds a terrible time. The birds decided not to let the jays drive them out. We had planted some large sunflower plants at the far edge of the field and covered the flower heads with cloth. The blue jays picked right through the cloth and ate the seeds as they became ready to eat.

One day we saw Robby come up on the deck and inspect his old nest. He found it was still there where he left it. We noticed he did a bit of window peeping at the same time. I still had all my canaries inside, and I knew he could hear them singing as he would listen. But he was never a bit jealous.

For their next nest, they went up into the tall elm in the backyard. We had much rain so we knew they would have no difficulty getting enough food for their little ones.

When it was time to migrate, they brought their whole family to tell us they were leaving. They waited for us to notice they were here, and then flew away.

They must not have gone too far away, because they came back occasionally to check on us.

Chapter Fourteen

One day I received a call from a man who lived up the mountain. He had picked up a little hummingbird that had apparently been abandoned by it's mother. He asked me if I wanted to come and get it. I decided to go and found it had a malformed wing and would never be normal. I did not know how long it would live. I did not know what else might be wrong with it.

A small canary cage was just the perfect place for it. For its perch I used a tiny piece of bamboo, just the right size for its tiny little feet. I purchased some special fortified food, and, along with the regular syrup, it seemed to get along just fine.

It was a precious little thing and really appreciated the care given to it. Each day I took the hummingbird with me for a walk. It tried to fly but landed in a heap, so was content to remain on my shoulder.

I kept the cage on the corner of the piano where I had to pass by frequently. When the little bird saw me coming, it would jump off the perch and roll over on its back, hoping I would take pity and pick it up and hold it. If I pretended not to notice, it would get back up on the perch until it saw me coming toward it again.

We had this tiny little bird about two or three months. One day I was holding it in my hand when I saw its eyes glaze over. I knew it had just come to the end of its little life. It had been a beautiful little friend.

By February 22, 1980, Robby was back to stay for the season. He called from the top of the pine tree, and when he knew we heard him, he came down to the lower branch to talk. Tom was in the garden, and Robby flew over where he was and had a good visit before he flew away.

This year he talked to us almost every day. Occasionally he stopped for a long talk, and other times he stayed just for a moment. March was cold with snow and wind, which Robby did not appreciate. But he and his mate had much time to play around in the wooded areas before making plans for a nest.

The mockingbird had returned and hoped to discourage Robby and his mate from staying with us. He was a beautiful singer, and we hoped they could both live in peace. We knew he would not allow Robby and his mate to nest in the backyard, so they built their nest in the big hemlock in the front yard.

The two birds must have reached an understanding. We often heard the mockingbird singing, and now he was not so aggressive. Robby was always very friendly and curious about our activities, especially if we did something different from what we usually did.

Food was scarce so all the birds feasted on the wild cherries and apples. The blue jays that lived in the woods across the creek constantly harassed the mockingbirds and Robby. The blue jays tried to chase all the other birds away from the area but did not succeed. The mockingbirds also persisted and refused to leave.

Robby was still with us on November 21, but would soon be leaving with his mate and this year's family.

Robby came back early, as the winter was short and unseasonably warm. He seemed to know when it was safe to be here and where to go when it was stormy and cold. He always let us know he had arrived, though he spent much of his time with the other robins. He had no particular responsibilities yet.

By March all the birds were staking claim on their territories. This year the mockingbird wanted the whole space for himself. He even claimed the front yard. Apparently, he did not want to share the berry patch with any other bird.

One day we heard Robby and the mockingbird arguing in the front yard. We had company, and we went outside with them as they were leaving. Robby thought we had come out just to help him with his problem. The mockingbird flew away and left the tree for Robby, so he flew up to a high branch and thanked us for helping him.

It was still early. The ground was very cold, and the worms were still under ground. The birds had to rely on berries still hanging on the trees. The cedar waxwings came in a group and settled in Robby's holly tree. Being outnumbered, he let them have the tree and flew over to the neighbor's yard to a bush which still had berries on it.

The next day we came out our back-door and heard Robby call for help. We found that the cedar waxwings were trying to take over his bush by the neighbor's house. Tom went over and chased them away. They got the message and went back to the holly tree, leaving Robby and his chosen bush alone.

By this time Robby's mate had arrived. They claimed our front yard plus the neighbor's. It had warmed up, and it was now possible to find worms. They liked the bird-bath in the neighbor's backyard and were there daily keeping clean and fresh.

He and his mate found it interesting when they saw us working with the chickens. Robby was not jealous and knew he was free to go wherever he chose to watch what we were doing.

Tom took a trailer over to a barnyard for a load of manure, and Robby went along to see what he was doing. Luckily for Robby and his mate, the manure was full of worms. He watched as Tom unloaded the trailer and put the car in the garage. Robby then sang his good-night song and went off to roost.

For their first nest, Robby and his mate built in the pine tree in the neighbor's yard. But something happened to this nest, for we saw broken eggs on the ground. For their next nest they chose to go into the spruce tree in our front yard. This was their second try, and again something tore the nest apart. They tried for a third time, but whatever was destroying their nest also ruined this one. Finally they gave up on an early nesting.

We had been having a lot of rain, so there were many worms for them to eat. Now the strawberry season was beginning, and this was a very welcome time of year. The mockingbirds, bobwhites, and other birds were there to get their share.

The summer was hot and very humid with a lot of rain. We didn't see where they built their next nest. Probably in the tall trees by the creek.

They stayed until late in the fall, finally leaving in November. They came back on December 6, so we felt they had not gone too far away.

They visited us frequently in January of 1982, coming back to stay in February, bringing last year's babies with them. This time they roosted in the big hemlock in our front yard. All settled for the night, they expected us to come outside to tell them good night. Then they were happy and quiet and went to sleep. But they woke up early every morning to sing their wake-up song for us. We didn't need an alarm clock, that's for sure.

Some days they flew off by themselves, visiting other places, and other times they stayed nearby. They were always full of curiosity. They thought everything we did was for their good in some way, so they often supervised us from their spot in the tree.

Late in July, Robby came to the kitchen door and called to me. When I went outside he led me down toward the garden and perched on a post. I wondered what he wanted, so looked around. There on a compost pile of leaves was his one little baby. He was so proud of it, and wanted me to see it. I walked very close but did not touch. I told him what a beautiful baby it was, with all the pretty spots on its breast. It was so fat and well cared for.

I went back to the kitchen. To my surprise, a few minutes later Tom came to the door with the baby bird in his hands. I wondered what Robby thought about that! But Robby was right behind him, approving of it. We took the baby bird outside just as

Robby's mate flew up. We knew by the way she acted that *she* did not want us touching her baby. They took the little one without problem and went their way.

We still had a big problem with the cats across the creek. Their owner was a "cat lover" and let them roam wherever they wanted to go. And there were quite a few of them! Sadly, one of the cats caught Robby's mate.

We were sure he couldn't find another mate so late in the season and were happily surprised when he came to us with a young mate a short time later.

We always had a flock of chickens that we kept in a coop and allowed to range in a fenced yard. We sold the hens in the spring, when the young pullets were about to begin laying. We always closed their door when they went to roost at night. They were controlled by a time clock that shut off the lights at a certain time. In the summer it was too warm to have the door shut, so we used a strong screen door to protect them. Many times during the early morning we would hear them fussing, only to find fox tracks outside their door.

In the early spring we would get the day-old pullets and brood them inside the building until they were able to be placed in an area outside to range. All of the chickens became pets. If a chicken got out of the yard, we would just open the gate and she would go in, or we would pick her up and put her back in. We always had two roosters in the flock that would warn the hens of any danger nearby.

We had a good patch of blueberries and blackberries, which we had to keep covered with a heavy net held in place by wires strung on posts. This way it protected the fruit from all the birds that would have feasted there.

Robby and his new mate began to nest in the trees across the creek, so we didn't see them as we'd done previously. Robby was as friendly as ever and watched us as closely as before. But his mate wanted to stay her distance.

During the fruit season, I watched the fruit patch closely, as the birds often got inside the fenced area. The brown thrashers gave us the greatest problem. Each day I went out to catch the birds that had gotten inside, and let them loose.

One day as I opened the gate to go in, Robby was in the tree above me. He tried to tell me something, and I soon found out what it was. One of his babies was inside the fenced fruit area. Robby sat in the tree and watched me catch his little one. Then he met me at the gate as I came out holding his baby. He then took the little one and flew off without showing a bit of fear. I wondered if he had helped the baby get inside to eat his fill of blueberries and blackberries, knowing it would not be harmed.

Chapter Fifteen

We had two roosters in the flock who were as different as night and day. One was very feisty, while the other was calm and quiet. One day a friend gave us a bantam rooster, and we put him in the yard with the other chickens. The bantam decided he would be the king of the group, so he soon picked a fight with the big rooster. We decided to take the quiet rooster out of the yard and see what would happen. It was not an even fight. When they bristled up for a fight, the little bantam disappeared between the legs of the big rooster and thoroughly confused him. When we traded the feisty rooster for the calm one, the little bantam thought he had won the fight. The quiet rooster didn't want to fight him and just walked away. We decided to find a new home for the bantam.

When we purchased our baby chicks, we noticed one little pullet was not all white like the rest, but had quite a few brown feathers on her body. The other chickens didn't like her because she was different and began to pick at her head. Sadly, after several days of this, she was badly hurt and became blind.

She was a good hen, so we fenced off a small place in the laying house for her. We gave her food and water, and she became used to her little place. She continued to lay an egg every day. When it was not raining, I'd take her outside and place her where she could pick greens, even if she could not see. She knew that after a time I would come to take her back to the coop. She recognized her name, and when we spoke to her she'd cluck in reply. We kept up this special treatment as long as we kept the flock of hens. We were still feeding them a vegetarian mash, so we had more requests for eggs than we could even handle. We found the flavor of the eggs was far better that that of eggs from hens fed mash made from meat scraps. Our hens were in better health, too.

Robby kept watch of everything that went on around the home. He and his new mate were nesting among the tall trees by the creek, so we were not aware of their family unless they brought them up for us to see. He still favored us with his early morning song and his daily companionship. He followed us wherever we went, so he could enjoy our friends like he always did.

We had gotten another bunch of baby chicks and had them in the outside yard, where they would live until they began to lay. Then we'd put them in the laying house. We had to watch carefully, as the neighbor's cat from across the creek liked to lay close to the fence, hoping to snatch a chicken for an easy meal.

Robby still came up and sat in the flowering crab apple tree so he could watch what was going on inside the house. He enjoyed watching me take care of the canaries that he could see through the glass deck doors. Each morning I spent at least half an hour cleaning and feeding them for the day. Once a week or more, depending on the weather, they had a bath, and Robby could see that from where he sat. Sometimes he came up on the deck rail for a closer look. I knew he could hear them sing and was willing to blend his song with theirs.

Tom and I went out one day, and when we came home all the birds were chirping loudly, as if something was badly wrong. I checked from cage to cage and soon found a cage door open and no bird inside. Hunting for it, I soon found it safely snuggled in a hanging plant. When I placed it back in its cage, the birds began to sing again. They knew the little one was not where it should be and let me know so I could put it back where it belonged.

Spring was a happy time when the canaries nested and raised their little ones. Before the season was over we would have over a hundred canaries. Sometimes my friends would call on the telephone and want to listen to the songs they could hear before telling me why they were calling.

The time came when Tom's health began to fail. His health had worsened over the years. One day I returned home from an appointment and found him where he had been reading. I thought he had fallen asleep in his chair, as he'd often done before. But this time he did not wake up. Although the doctors had warned me that this might happen, it was hard to accept. Now I was alone.

I kept the chickens for a while, but the work of carrying feed was too heavy, so I decided to sell them. First I sold the laying hens. When people saw how tame and quiet they were, I had ready buyers. Next I had to let the pullets go.

One man came in the afternoon and wanted a couple dozen. It was daytime, and he told me that he knew it would be hard for me to catch them in the daylight, since they could see me coming. He offered to come into the yard and help me corner the chickens. Instead, I asked him to stay outside and point to the ones he wanted. He didn't think I could catch them alone, but he did as I asked.

He pointed to a certain hen, and I walked over and picked her up and handed her to him. This was the way he chose the hens he wanted. The next day he was back for more. He said they were the quietest chickens he had ever had. Soon all were sold.

Robby noticed that Tom was not around as usual. He called for him and looked all over for him. He knew something had happened, but could not figure it out. But he soon got used to Tom being gone, and watched me and sang as he always had.

It was springtime, and I still didn't know where Robby and his mate had built their nest. His mate wouldn't let them build close to our home. I missed that very much, but I knew they had a mind of their own and did as they pleased.

Time passed and I decided to fly to the West Coast. I know Robby wondered what had happened to me, but when I came back, he was there to let me know he was glad I had returned.

More time passed, and I decided to get married again. I left after Robby and his mate migrated, so they did not miss me until they returned. My husband, Alfred, and I returned in the spring, and Robby was there to welcome us back. I am sure he searched all over and could not find me. He watched closely to make sure we did not leave him again, and was there each day to sing for us.

A year or so later we moved to a different home, and Robby watched as we made the transfer and flew along to make sure he knew just where we were. He was there every day to sing and wanted us to let him know we knew he was there.

Our new home was surrounded by mountains and many tall trees, so we didn't know if Robby stayed nearby or went back to his old area. We just knew he found time to visit us and to make sure we had not moved again.

We enjoyed planting a garden, as we had two acres at this place. It was a pleasure to have our own vegetables, fresh from the garden to the table. Being so close to the woods, we had many different animals and birds who enjoyed the wonderful food also. We planted more than we needed, hoping they would leave enough for us.

We planted a good-sized patch of soy beans, which was very much appreciated by the rabbits. We managed to get our share to put in the freezer. We didn't plant strawberries, which, I am sure, was a disappointment to Robby.

My husband needed somewhere to store all his machinery, so his next project was to build a shop. Robby was fascinated and kept watch as he worked. He'd perch in one of the nearby trees and watch as long as he wished, singing his cheery song and stopping to "talk" now and then.

Hedges and a hemlock tree grew near the house. These made perfect nesting places for the song sparrows and purple finches. Robby had noticed that each morning I walked down the hill about a block for the morning paper. He would perch in one of the trees along the lane and let me know he was there by calling or singing his morning song.

We had many flowers at our new home. We were surrounded on two sides by the wild rhododendron that grew and blossomed in the spring. Besides that, many dogwood and redbud trees bloomed very early. We really enjoyed the privacy the wooded area provided.

But time passes all too quickly. Again I found myself alone. The shock of losing Alfred so quickly was great, and time alone was not easy. I did find consolation in the things of nature around me. I noticed the little lizards that lived in the hedges by the front door. The female was very shy, but the male was a bit daring. He would come up on the porch rail to sun himself and dare me to come close to him. She would run away, but the male would stay until I was about a foot from him, and then he would run away also.

Chapter Sixteen

One day as I sat indoors reading, I heard a strange noise on my front window screen. I went outside to see what was making the noise and found a tiny, baby grey squirrel.

I knew it would not have been out of its nest at that early age if its mother was still alive. She let me pick her up with no problem, so I knew she must be very hungry. I had a very small cage that I had used to carry canaries in. It was just the right size for a temporary squirrel nest. I fixed up a milk drink for her, and she clung to the spoon and drank it all. I knew I could not let her loose as she would not survive, so made plans to keep her. It was September, so I knew I'd have her all winter. I called her Babe. She was so tiny I could hold her in the palm of one hand and cover her with my other hand.

I went downtown to get a cage that would be large enough so she would be able to exercise. At the same time I bought some kitten formula for her. I couldn't find anything to bottle-feed her with, so I just let her drink from the spoon. That was no problem, as she'd grasp the spoon with her very nimble fingers and hold it until all the milk was gone.

I called a nature center to get some advice and information in general about baby squirrels. She proved to be a very pleasant pet for me during the winter months.

As she grew, I took her outside when the weather was nice. She did not like wind or the cold and would quickly get inside my jacket. I always wore slacks and a heavy shirt to protect me from her claws. Babe's favorite spot was by the window above the kitchen sink, where she could see out and watch the other squirrels play in the trees.

If she was not in her cage when someone came to the front door, she would hide inside my jacket and sometimes go down the sleeve. One day a man came to the door asking directions for someone, and she stuck her head out of the sleeve. Needless to say, the man was shocked, as that was the last thing he expected to see.

If we were alone, I would let her loose to get some exercise. She always stayed close to me. If I was in my chair reading, she would run around and around on my chair, stopping just long enough to rub my nose as she raced by. I always wore clothes that covered me well, for her claws were so sharp. She liked to climb up to my shoulders. If for some reason I wasn't well covered, I'd just collapse until I could get a hold on her. She liked to be covered by my jacket or go down the sleeve. She felt it was her special hiding place.

In the fall I'd bought a good supply of almonds in the shell. This was Babe's favorite food, along with shelled pecans. She did not like peanuts and would not eat bird seed. I gave her some sunflower seeds, but she would rather have the nuts. She liked to hide her almonds under the throw rugs. When I saw a lump under a rug, I knew it was a nut she had hidden, and I would take it back to her cage.

Babe was very clean. When I sat down to eat my dinner, she would come to see what I had on my plate. She especially liked green beans, so if I had some, she would daintily pick up one and take it away to eat it.

She had her special places where she liked to play in the dark. One was in the cupboard above the refrigerator. I put her favorite toys in there so she could go there if she chose. I kept wooden things in her cage so she could chew and chew to her heart's content. Her favorite thing was a wooden spoon. She had that chewed beyond recognition.

Babe did not like men. When I knew someone was coming, I would be sure she was in her cage. If a man came close to her cage, she would act as if she would like to eat him alive. One day a repairman asked me how I could take care of such a vicious animal. I went over and put my arm in the cage, and all she did was play with my fingers. She knew I was her caregiver, and I had no problem.

On sunny days, I'd take Babe outside and let her play on the ground. But I had a hard time getting her to climb trees. One day she was on my shoulder when I took her for a walk, and a truck made a big noise that scared her. In fright, she jumped off my shoulder and ran up a nearby tree.

That was her first experience in a tree.

After that, I took her out every nice day, and she spent her day playing around high up in the tree. When evening came, I'd call her down so she could be indoors for the night. The first time or two she came down and got on my shoulder and went to the house with me. After that, she went by herself and beat me to the front door.

One nice day she did not come to be let in for the night and spent a few nights outside. I knew she was missing her regular food and water, so I left the door ajar, and she came in by herself. I heard her trying to get water at the sink. She was glad to be inside again.

After that, she made sure she was not outside overnight. She had some hairs pulled out of her tail, so I think she met up with some attacker that frightened her very much. After her time out of the house, she kept snuggling in my sleeve. She could not get enough attention—she just stayed with me and purred loudly. She wanted to stay with me until she was tucked in her bed for the night.

Babe knew when she was being corrected. She would stand on her haunches with her hands folded and look at me. Sometimes I'd see that she was tempted to chew something she knew she shouldn't. I'd say, "No, No!" and she would go do something else. She liked to play with empty paper bags or egg cartons. She would follow me wherever I went, so I had to be careful not to shut a door on her.

When she was in her cage and I did not want her to get out, I had to wire the door shut. Soon she found how to untwist the wire with her fingers. After that I had to put a weight on top of the cage, so even if she got the wire loose, she could not lift the door.

During the winter she would go to the door and stand there, hoping I would take her outside. So I went outside and brought back a pan full of snow. Then I put her in it, so she would know what snow was. She wanted no part of it and was content to look out the window after that!

When she was small, I gave her a plastic ice-cream pail to sleep in. She chewed and chewed on the sides of the pail until it was chewed to the bottom. Altogether, she chewed down five pails before she was able to sleep without her special bed. Later she was content just to cover up with a towel and sleep on another towel that I gave her.

If she found a box of facial tissue, she'd pull each one out of the box—if I did not find her first. She'd carry it all to her bed to make it soft for her afternoon nap. When she napped, she used her tail for a cover. Since she had spent time outside at night, she had not wanted to chew everything so much.

Her hearing was very good, and I found it impossible to slip up on her. I was very careful not to let her catch me with my bare feet or my toes really got it! I learned to keep things out of her way. Babe just loved pencils and keys and once she had them, she didn't want to give them up. I had to coax her with something else before she would let me have whatever it was I needed.

I gave her a Brazil nut one day. It was the first time she had ever had one, and she really liked it. Once she had a piece of chocolate candy, but hated it.

She'd often lay on the counter, and as I passed by I would rub her back. She liked that very much.

One day I was on the telephone and she slipped into the bathroom and came out with a trail of toilet tissue following her. She was my constant companion and even tried to hide a nut down my neck. One day I put on a pair of gloves. She'd never seen that before and thought she could have some fun—with all four feet!

She had learned the routine and knew that as soon as breakfast was over I cleaned her cage and gave her a new supply of nuts.

In February, Robby called to me so I would know he was back from the Southland. It was good to hear his happy song again. He was waiting for me when I went after the newspaper in the morning, as he had always done before.

I sold this house and had to pack everything again. Robby had been coming to see me regularly, insisting on long conversations. He had not had a chance to fill me in on his winter vacation yet and felt it was important that he do so. I just wished I could understand him.

I thought Babe was not feeling well, so I put a heating pad under her cage so it would be warm for her to sleep on. She must have gotten chilled when she was outside. I began to give her vitamins, and she soon felt better. It had been rainy and cold that one day, and she always hated the wind, rain, and cold weather.

Before I put her in her bed for the night, I would hold her on my shoulder, pet her, and rock her for a while. She got so spoiled that she would not settle down in her cage until I took her out and rocked her.

Robby came every day. He could see something was going on that he couldn't understand. When the big moving van arrived, he knew I was moving again. He stayed and watched to see where I was going—just a few miles away. He flew there to watch us unload.

I put Babe's cage outside on the front patio so she could get used to the new area. I took her for walks and let her look around, but did not let her loose. I knew when she left me now, it would be for good. There were no trees near my new home for her to climb.

One morning as I went outside for the newspaper, I found Robby checking the flower garden for worms. When I opened the door, he walked out on the drive and burst into full song, then flew away. I was happy to learn that he knew this was my new home.

Many times he would call from a tree some distance away and wait until I spotted him, and then, would fly away.

One day as I was parking my car nearby, he called to me. I followed the sound of his call until I stood under the branch where he was perched. We had another good conversation. This was one of the few times he came up close, because there were few trees nearby.

When I decided to take a short course at a nearby college, I didn't give any thought to Robby. But when I arrived at the parking lot, locked the car, and turned to go to my class, Robby called to me from a branch just over my head. He was so glad I had seen him. He flipped his tail, and we had a good conversation, which satisfied him. He wanted me to know he had been following me there each day.

By this time, I had let Babe go into the woods. She was gone about a week before I saw her again. She had discovered a place where she could get sunflower seeds to eat and came every day. One day I came along as she was coming to eat. She climbed the tree and lay on the branch just over my head. She stayed there listening to me talk to her, but didn't come down to me. She had gotten used to being free and wanted to stay that way. Another time, she stood on her haunches like she always had when she waited at the door to be let outside. When she knew I was watching she climbed the tree and showed me how much fun she had playing in the branches. She made sure I was watching her all the time.

Later I saw her coming to eat, bringing

two little babies with her. She had a life of her own now and was satisfied with it. I have seen her on occasions, and she has let me know she recognized me, but is satisfied with her freedom.

Robby called to me before he migrated in 1995. I eagerly waited to see if he would come back in the spring. He was now 26 years and 6 months old.

When spring came, I kept watch, hoping to hear his cheery call, but it was not to be. He didn't come back. Robby left me many pleasant memories. I still find myself listening for his call.

Having Robby, Babe, and so many of God's creatures with me has been like a little glimpse of heaven.